Landform Top Tens

The World's Most Amazing Volcanoes

Anna Claybourne

www.raintreepublishers.co.uk
Visit our website to find out
more information about
Raintree books.

To order:
☎ Phone +44 (0) 1865 888066
▤ Fax +44 (0) 1865 314091
▨ Visit www.raintreepublishers.co.uk

Raintree is an imprint of **Capstone Global Library Limited**, a company incorporated in England and Wales having its registered office at 7 Pilgrim Street, London, EC4V 6LB – Registered company number: 6695582

"Raintree" is a registered trademark of Pearson Education Limited, under licence to Capstone Global Library Limited

Text © Capstone Global Library Limited 2009
First published in hardback in 2009
The moral rights of the proprietor have been asserted.

Edited by Louise Galpine, Kate DeVilliers, and Rachel Howells
Designed by Victoria Bevan and Geoff Ward
Original illustrations © Capstone Global Library Limited
Illustrated by Geoff Ward
Picture research by Hannah Taylor
Production by Alison Parsons
Originated by Modern Age Repro House Ltd.
Printed and bound in China by CTPS

ISBN 978 1 406211 00 9 (hardback)
13 12 11 10 09
10 9 8 7 6 5 4 3 2 1

British Library Cataloguing in Publication Data

Claybourne, Anna
The world's most amazing volcanoes. - (Landform top tens)
551.2'1
A full catalogue record for this book is available from the British Library.

Acknowledgements

We would like to thank the following for permission to reproduce photographs: Alamy p. **15** (Emmanuel LATTES); California Institute of Technology, Pasadena, CA p. **26** (Courtesy of Dr. MJ Mahoney); Corbis pp. **14**, **25** (Charles O'Rear); Getty Images pp. **16** (Sisse Brimberg and Cotton Coulson), **19** (Science Faction/ Ed Darack), **27** (National Geographic/ Karen Kasmauski); Photolibrary pp. **8** (Pacific Stock/ Peter French), **9** (Pacific Stock/ Ron Dahlquist), **10** (DEA/ S Vannini), **11** (Robert Harding Travel/ Walter Rawlings), **12** (Animals Animals/ David Boyle), **17** (OSF/ Richard Packwood), **18** (Tips Italia/ Luciano Lepre), **20** (JTB Photo), **21** (Imagestate/ Steve Vidler), **22** (Corbis), **23** (Purestock); Science Photo Library pp. **4–5** (Dr Juerg Alean), **6–7** (NASA), **13** (Jeremy Bishop).

Background images by Getty Images (Photodisc) and Capstone Global Library Ltd (Debbie Rowe).

Cover photograph of Kilauea Volcano, reproduced with permission of Rex Features (Stock Connection/ Douglas Peebles).

We would like to thank Nick Lapthorn for his invaluable help in the preparation of this book.

Every effort has been made to contact copyright holders of material reproduced in this book. Any omissions will be rectified in subsequent printings if notice is given to the publishers.

Disclaimer

Contents

Some words are printed in bold, **like this**. You can find out what they mean by looking in the glossary on page 31.

Volcanoes

A volcano is an opening in Earth's surface where red-hot liquid rock escapes from under the ground. Volcanoes can also throw out hot gases, hot ash, or solid rocks. When this happens, it is called an **eruption**.

How volcanoes work

Deep inside Earth, it is very hot. Some of the rock there is **molten** and runny. Where there are cracks in Earth's surface, the hot, liquid rock, called **lava**, can escape. As it comes out, it cools, hardens, and piles up, creating a mountain shape. Many of the world's most famous mountains are volcanoes.

Some volcanoes erupt with a big bang. They are called **stratovolcanoes**, and often have a tall, pointy shape. Slow, gentle eruptions create wide **shield volcanoes**. Frequent, small eruptions make a cone-shaped pile of lava, called a **cinder cone volcano**.

Volcanoes can be **active**, if they still erupt, or **extinct**, if they have stopped erupting. If a volcano is quiet, but could erupt again one day, it is **inactive** or **dormant**.

Stromboli in Italy flings out lava, ash, and red-hot rocks as it erupts.

Friends or foes?

Volcanoes are dangerous. A big eruption can destroy towns and kill many people. However, volcanoes can be helpful too. Ash and lava from eruptions makes soil very **fertile**. Volcanoes also attract tourists, helping local people to make a living.

Tambora

When Mount Tambora in Indonesia exploded on 10 April 1815, it was the biggest volcanic **eruption** in history! The booming sound could be heard more than 2,500 km (1,500 miles) away. It was also one of the deadliest eruptions ever. Around 70,000 people were killed by the flows of **lava,** hot ash, and gas.

The year without a summer

The eruption of Mount Tambora filled the sky with so much dust and ash, it blocked out a lot of sunlight. This made the world's weather very cold for over a year. 1816 was called "the year without a summer".

Building up pressure

Tambora is a **stratovolcano** – a volcano that erupts suddenly. Inside it is a space called a **magma chamber**. In the years leading up to 1815, the chamber filled up with sticky **magma** (**molten** rock) from inside Earth. Eventually, it was bulging and ready to burst. In 1812, the volcano began to rumble. Then, in 1815, it finally erupted.

This satellite image shows the area around Tambora today. The volcano is towards the top left of the image.

MOUNT TAMBORA

LOCATION:
INDONESIA, ASIA

TYPE OF VOLCANO:
STRATOVOLCANO

STATUS:
ACTIVE

HEIGHT:
2,851 METRES (9,354 FT)

THAT'S AMAZING!:
BEFORE 1815, TAMBORA WAS OVER 4,000 METRES (13,100 FT) HIGH. THE ERUPTION BLEW OVER 1,000 METRES (3,281 FT) OFF ITS TOP!

ASIA

Pacific
Ocean

Indian
Ocean

INDONESIA

Mount Tambora

Kilauea

Kilauea, on Big Island in Hawaii, is one of the most **active** volcanoes in the world. This volcano has been **erupting** constantly since 1983. It hasn't stopped for over 25 years!

Tourists stand back to watch hot lava flowing and cooling on Kilauea.

Going slow

Kilauea is a **shield volcano**. It rarely erupts with a big bang. Instead, it has very runny **lava** that flows gently from cracks or **vents**. The lava runs down the volcano's sides, and cools and hardens to build up a rounded shield shape.

Because Kilauea is on an island, some of the lava flows all the way down its sides and into the sea. It crackles and pops as it touches the cold seawater. The lava usually flows slowly, so tourists can climb Kilauea quite safely.

Lava from Kilauea enters the sea, making the water boil and steam.

Vesuvius

Vesuvius, in Italy, is one of the most dangerous volcanoes in the world. It is a **stratovolcano**, so it has sudden, powerful **eruptions**. It towers over the busy city of Naples, which means an eruption could cause disaster. Almost three million people live close enough to Vesuvius to be at risk from a big eruption.

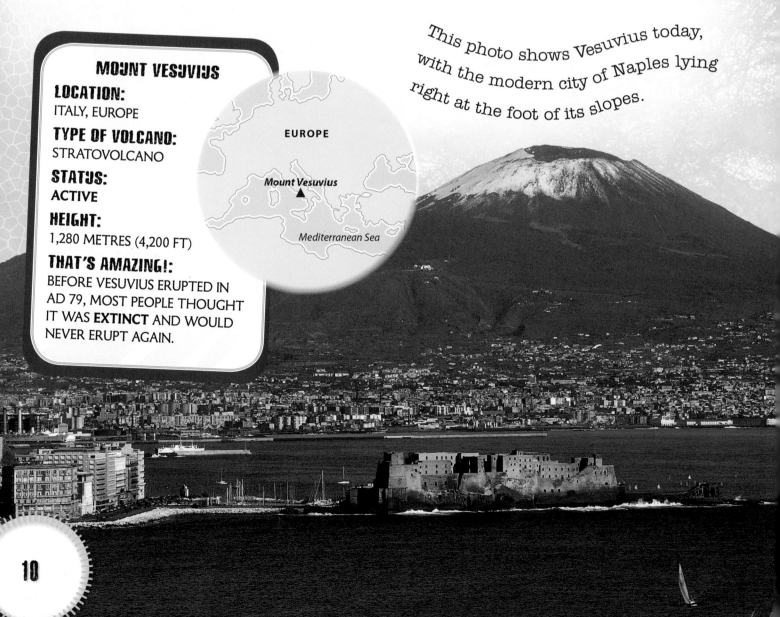

This photo shows Vesuvius today, with the modern city of Naples lying right at the foot of its slopes.

MOUNT VESUVIUS

LOCATION:
ITALY, EUROPE

TYPE OF VOLCANO:
STRATOVOLCANO

STATUS:
ACTIVE

HEIGHT:
1,280 METRES (4,200 FT)

THAT'S AMAZING!:
BEFORE VESUVIUS ERUPTED IN AD 79, MOST PEOPLE THOUGHT IT WAS **EXTINCT** AND WOULD NEVER ERUPT AGAIN.

EUROPE

Mount Vesuvius ▲

Mediterranean Sea

Ancient eruption

Vesuvius has already shown how deadly it can be. Its most famous eruption, in the year AD 79, destroyed two ancient Roman cities, Pompeii and Herculaneum, and killed over 2,000 people.

The AD 79 eruption trapped its victims under hot ash, which hardened to leave body-shaped moulds.

Pyroclastic flows

In AD 79, many of Vesuvius' victims were caught in **pyroclastic flows**. These are fast-moving flows of rock, dust, and hot gas that rush down the sides of erupting stratovolcanoes. Pyroclastic flows are rare – but when they do happen, they are deadly.

Mount St. Helens

In 1980, Mount St. Helens, in the United States, **erupted**. It was the biggest ever volcanic disaster to occur in the United States. The top of the volcano collapsed, making it 400 metres (1,313 ft) lower than it had been. A huge area of forest and farmland was covered with ash and rock. Roads, railways, and homes were destroyed, and thousands of animals died.

This is Mount St. Helens after its famous 1980 eruption.

MOUNT ST. HELENS

LOCATION:
WASHINGTON STATE, USA, NORTH AMERICA

TYPE OF VOLCANO:
STRATOVOLCANO

STATUS:
ACTIVE

HEIGHT:
2,550 METRES (8,365 FT)

THAT'S AMAZING!:
83-YEAR-OLD INNKEEPER HARRY R. TRUMAN REFUSED TO LEAVE HIS HOME AT THE FOOT OF MOUNT ST. HELENS, AND DIED IN THE ERUPTION. TODAY A NEARBY **RIDGE** IS NAMED AFTER HIM.

NORTH AMERICA

Mount St. Helens

Pacific Ocean

Atlantic Ocean

A volcanologist uses a camcorder to film a **lava** flow in action.

Warning signs

Scientists knew the volcano was about to blow, because it had started to bulge and tremble. A mass of **magma** was pushing upwards inside it. Most local people managed to escape in time, but a few weren't so lucky. A **volcanologist** (volcano scientist) named David Johnston was killed while studying the eruption. In total, 57 people died.

Paricutin

Most of the world's volcanoes formed long before human history began. However, one amazing volcano seems to have come from nowhere. The **cinder cone volcano** Paricutin, in Mexico, first appeared one day in 1943. Farmer Dionisio Pulido was working in his fields when he saw smoke and ash pouring out of a crack in the ground. The volcano grew and grew, covering nearby villages with **lava** and ash.

An onlooker watches Paricutin **erupt** and grow in this photo from the 1950s.

Today, Paricutin is no longer erupting.
It will probably never erupt again.

Growing up

Over the next nine years, Paricutin became a cone-shaped
hill 424 metres (1,390 ft) high. As it formed on high ground,
its peak is now 3,170 metres (10,400 ft) above sea level. Like
other cinder cone volcanoes, it is a straight-sided heap of
volcanic rock and ash. At the top is a large, wide **crater**
– the opening where the lava came out.

Kilimanjaro

Kilimanjaro, in Tanzania, is the highest mountain in Africa. It is also one of the world's biggest isolated volcanoes. That means it stands on its own in a flat plain, instead of being part of a **range** of other mountains. It has three volcanic peaks, each with its own **crater**. Kilimanjaro is a **dormant** volcano, and is not currently **erupting**. But it does release jets of gas and steam, called **fumaroles**, and it could one day erupt again.

This aerial photograph shows Kilimanjaro's summit, with snow around its crater.

KILIMANJARO

LOCATION:
TANZANIA, AFRICA

TYPE OF VOLCANO:
STRATOVOLCANO

STATUS:
DORMANT

HEIGHT:
5,895 METRES (19,341 FT)

THAT'S AMAZING!:
BECAUSE IT IS SO HIGH, KILIMANJARO HAS SNOW ON ITS HIGHEST PEAKS – EVEN THOUGH IT STANDS ALMOST ON THE **EQUATOR**, WHERE THE WORLD IS HOTTEST.

AFRICA

Kilimanjaro

Atlantic Ocean

Indian Ocean

This is a view of Kilimanjaro from the African **savannah**.

Tourist attraction

Kilimanjaro is famous for its stunning beauty. Tourists and climbers flock to its steep slopes and **summit** craters. It has traditionally been a holy mountain for local people. According to legend, it is home to friendly spirits.

Ojos del Salado

Have you heard of Ojos del Salado? Most people haven't, yet it is one of the highest volcanoes in the world.

Wherever they are found, the height of volcanoes, like mountains, is measured from the surface of the sea, as this is roughly the same everywhere. Ojos del Salado, on the border between Argentina and Chile, stands 6,891 metres (22,609 ft) above sea level. That's over three-quarters of the height of Mount Everest, the highest mountain in the world.

Crater lakes

Ojos del Salado is home to one of the world's highest lakes, Laguna Verde (meaning "Green Lake"). It is a **crater lake** – a lake that collects in a volcano's **crater**.

Will it blow again?

Scientists aren't sure whether Ojos del Salado is **active** or **dormant**. It hasn't **erupted** properly for over a thousand years, but it does give out steam. This means that there is still hot, **molten** rock, and boiling water somewhere inside it.

This hut is used by climbers of Ojos del Salado.

Pacific Ocean

SOUTH AMERICA

Atlantic Ocean

Ojos del Salado

Mount Fuji

When you think of a perfect volcano, you probably think of a volcano like Mount Fuji. It is one of the best-known volcanoes on Earth. It is also the highest mountain in Japan, and has been a symbol of Japan for centuries. It features in many well-known Japanese paintings.

MOUNT FUJI

LOCATION:
JAPAN, ASIA

TYPE OF VOLCANO:
STRATOVOLCANO

STATUS:
DORMANT

HEIGHT:
3,776 METRES
(12,388 FT)

THAT'S AMAZING!:
UNTIL THE 1860S, WOMEN WEREN'T ALLOWED TO GO TO THE TOP OF MOUNT FUJI!

ASIA

▲ Mount Fuji

Pacific Ocean

Mount Fuji often appears in Japanese art and poetry. This painting of it is by the great Japanese artist, Hokusai.

Triangle peak

Mount Fuji is a **stratovolcano**. It has a very smooth, triangular shape, with slightly concave (inward-curving) sides. It usually has a snowy top and dark lower slopes, making it easy to recognise.

Fuji has not **erupted** for several hundred years. It is very safe to climb, and around 200,000 climbers and tourists reach the top every year. It is also used for paragliding, skiing, and other sports.

Mount Fuji's perfect triangular shape towers above the city of Fujiyoshida.

Mauna Loa

Mauna Loa is the world's widest volcano. It is not the highest, but it takes up the most space. It is a massive **shield volcano** on Big Island in Hawaii, in the Pacific Ocean. It covers an area of about 5,200 km² (2,000 sq miles).

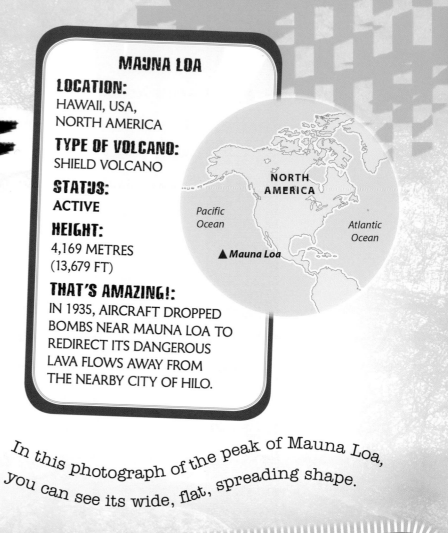

MAUNA LOA

LOCATION:
HAWAII, USA, NORTH AMERICA

TYPE OF VOLCANO:
SHIELD VOLCANO

STATUS:
ACTIVE

HEIGHT:
4,169 METRES (13,679 FT)

THAT'S AMAZING!:
IN 1935, AIRCRAFT DROPPED BOMBS NEAR MAUNA LOA TO REDIRECT ITS DANGEROUS LAVA FLOWS AWAY FROM THE NEARBY CITY OF HILO.

NORTH AMERICA

Pacific Ocean

Atlantic Ocean

▲ Mauna Loa

In this photograph of the peak of Mauna Loa, you can see its wide, flat, spreading shape.

Volcano chain

Volcano chain

The islands of Hawaii formed from a **hot spot** – a weak point in Earth's crust. Volcanoes **erupting** from this spot on the seabed grew so large that they reached the surface of the ocean. Over time, they have created a chain of volcanic islands.

This photo of Hawaii seen from space shows how its islands form a curved chain.

Shaping a shield

Like its neighbour, Kilauea (see pages 8-9), Mauna Loa has very runny **lava**. It flows a long way before cooling and hardening, and this is what gives Mauna Loa its extremely wide shield shape.

Krakatau

Krakatau in Indonesia is one of the world's most famous volcanoes. It is also one of the most **active** and violent. This island volcano has **erupted** many times in human history, and caused many deaths.

The big one

Krakatau's most famous eruption happened in 1883. On 27 August, the volcano blew apart in a huge eruption, and most of it collapsed into the sea. The eruption killed over 36,000 people in the surrounding area. But most of them weren't burned by **lava** or flattened by rocks and ash. Instead, they were drowned by **tsunamis** – giant waves created when rock from the exploding volcano plunged into the sea. Volcanoes by the sea, or on islands, can often cause deadly tsunamis.

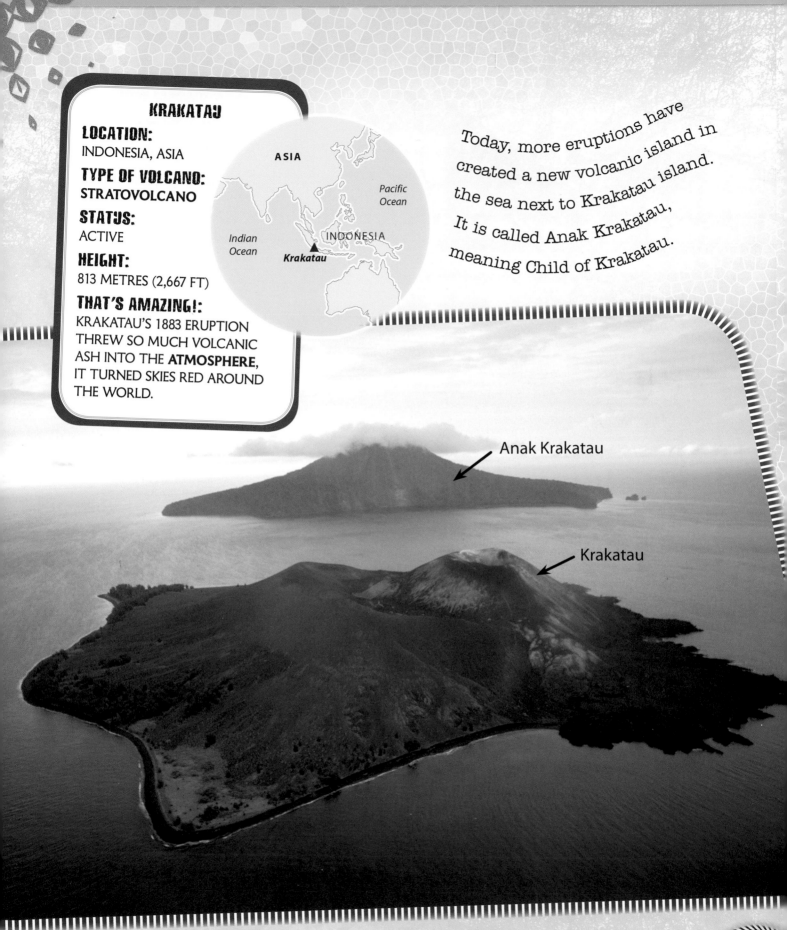

KRAKATAU

LOCATION:
INDONESIA, ASIA

TYPE OF VOLCANO:
STRATOVOLCANO

STATUS:
ACTIVE

HEIGHT:
813 METRES (2,667 FT)

THAT'S AMAZING!:
KRAKATAU'S 1883 ERUPTION THREW SO MUCH VOLCANIC ASH INTO THE **ATMOSPHERE**, IT TURNED SKIES RED AROUND THE WORLD.

ASIA

Pacific Ocean

Indian Ocean

INDONESIA

Krakatau

Today, more eruptions have created a new volcanic island in the sea next to Krakatau island. It is called Anak Krakatau, meaning Child of Krakatau.

Anak Krakatau

Krakatau

Volcanoes in danger

People are in danger from volcanoes **erupting**. But volcanoes are also in danger from us. Humans, especially tourists and climbers, can damage volcano areas, and the wild plants and animals that live there. When people visit or climb volcanoes, they often leave waste and litter, and disturb natural **habitats**. Thousands of people trekking up and down a volcano can also **erode** tracks and hillsides.

Many volcanoes are home to rare mountain wildlife. This is the Poás squirrel, which is only found on Volcan Poás.

Hikers gather on Mount Fuji's **summit** after completing the climb to the top.

Volcano national parks

Some countries protect their popular volcanoes by making the area around them into a national park or wildlife reserve. For example, Volcan Poás in Costa Rica, an **active stratovolcano,** has its own national park. Wardens patrol the area, guarding wildlife and picking up litter. Tourists are directed along specially built footpaths, and watch the volcano's **crater** from safe viewing platforms.

Volcano facts and figures

Volcanoes come in different shapes and sizes, and behave in different ways. Some are huge, but quiet and gentle; others are explosive, noisy, and dangerous. Which volcano do you think is the most amazing?

This map of the world shows all the volcanoes described in this book.

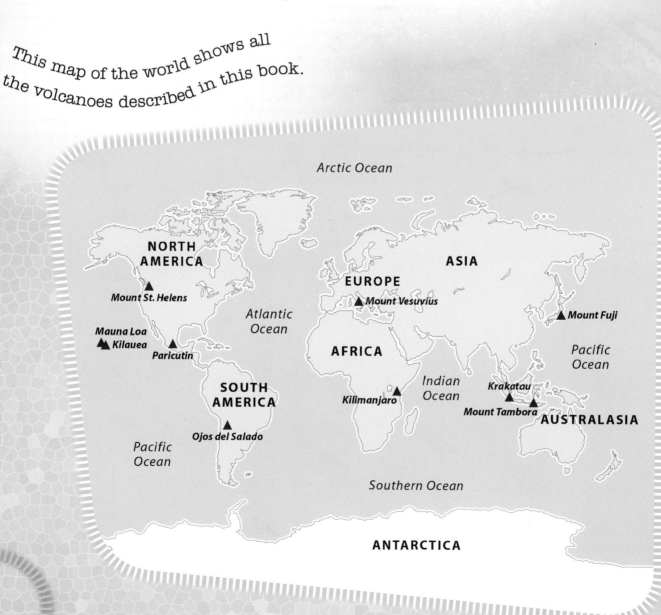

Arctic Ocean

NORTH AMERICA

Mount St. Helens

Mauna Loa
Kilauea

Paricutin

Atlantic Ocean

SOUTH AMERICA

Ojos del Salado

Pacific Ocean

EUROPE
Mount Vesuvius

ASIA

AFRICA

Kilimanjaro

Indian Ocean

Mount Fuji

Pacific Ocean

Krakatau

Mount Tambora

AUSTRALASIA

Southern Ocean

ANTARCTICA

MOUNT TAMBORA

TYPE OF VOLCANO:
STRATOVOLCANO

STATUS:
ACTIVE

HEIGHT:
2,851 METRES
(9,354 FT)

KILAUEA

TYPE OF VOLCANO:
SHIELD VOLCANO

STATUS:
ACTIVE

HEIGHT:
1,247 METRES
(4,091 FT)

MOUNT VESUVIUS

TYPE OF VOLCANO:
STRATOVOLCANO

STATUS:
ACTIVE

HEIGHT:
1,280 METRES
(4,200 FT)

MOUNT ST. HELENS

TYPE OF VOLCANO:
STRATOVOLCANO

STATUS:
ACTIVE

HEIGHT:
2,550 METRES
(8,365 FT)

PARICUTIN

TYPE OF VOLCANO:
CINDER CONE

STATUS:
EXTINCT

HEIGHT:
3,170 METRES
(10,400 FT)

KILIMANJARO

TYPE OF VOLCANO:
STRATOVOLCANO

STATUS:
DORMANT

HEIGHT:
5,895 METRES
(19,341 FT)

OJOS DEL SALADO

TYPE OF VOLCANO:
STRATOVOLCANO

STATUS:
EITHER DORMANT
OR ACTIVE

HEIGHT:
6,893 METRES
(22,616 FT)

MOUNT FUJI

TYPE OF VOLCANO:
STRATOVOLCANO

STATUS:
DORMANT

HEIGHT:
3,776 METRES
(12,388 FT)

MAUNA LOA

TYPE OF VOLCANO:
SHIELD VOLCANO

STATUS:
ACTIVE

HEIGHT:
4,169 METRES
(13,679 FT)

KRAKATAU

TYPE OF VOLCANO:
STRATOVOLCANO

STATUS:
ACTIVE

HEIGHT:
813 METRES
(2,667 FT)

Find out more

Books to read

Into the Volcano: A Volcano Researcher at Work, Donna O'Meara (Kids Can Press, 2007)

Mapping Earthforms: Volcanoes, Melanie Waldron (Heinemann Library, 2007)

Volcanoes, Anna Claybourne (Kingfisher, 2007)

Volcanoes, Stephanie Turnbull (Usborne Publishing, 2007)

Websites

Baking Soda Volcano
www.enchantedlearning.com/crafts/nature/volcano
Instructions for making your own erupting volcano model.

Discovery Volcano Explorer
http://kids.discovery.com/games/pompeii/pompeii.html
Amazing interactive graphics to help you understand more about volcanoes.

Interactives: Volcanoes
www.learner.org/interactives/volcanoes
Fascinating introduction to volcano science, with video clips of **lava** flows and other exciting volcanic events.

Volcano!
www.nationalgeographic.com/ngkids/0312/main.html
National Geographic's volcano site for kids, with animations and eruption videos.

Glossary

active active volcanoes erupt often, or show signs of volcanic activity

atmosphere gases surrounding Earth

cinder cone volcano cone-shaped volcano made of ash and rocks

crater bowl-shaped opening at the top of a volcano

crater lake lake that forms in a volcano's crater

dormant when volcanoes are quiet, but could erupt again

equator imaginary line around the middle of Earth

erode wear away

eruption when lava, ash, or rock bursts out of a volcano

extinct when volcanoes have stopped erupting and might never erupt again

fertile fertile land is rich and good for growing crops

fumarole jet of steam and gas from a crack in a volcano

habitat where a plant or animal lives

hot spot weak area in Earth's crust where volcanoes can form

inactive another word for "dormant"

lava liquid, molten rock that comes out of a volcano

magma name for molten rock when it is still inside Earth

magma chamber space under a volcano where magma collects

molten another word for "melted"

pyroclastic flow fast-moving flow of hot rocks, ash, and gas that forms during some eruptions

range row or group of mountains

ridge long, narrow peak often found in mountain areas

savannah flat, wide grasslands

shield volcano wide volcano formed by lava spreading out before it cools and hardens

stratovolcano tall, pointed volcano formed by a build-up of thick, sticky lava

summit top of a volcano

tsunami powerful wave caused by something making seawater move suddenly

vent channel that carries magma from inside a volcano to its crater or surface

volcanologist scientist who studies volcanoes

volcanology study of volcanoes

Index